Grand Marronage

Irène Mathieu

ISBN: 978-0-9861876-6-7
Library of Congress Control Number: 2018965220

Cover image: Irène Mathieu
Cover silhouette: Wikimedia Commons, Mrr catman
Cover and interior design: Alyse Knorr

Switchback Books
Kate Partridge and Alyse Knorr, Editors
editors@switchbackbooks.com
www.switchbackbooks.com

Praise for *Grand Marronage*

Grand Marronage is a remarkable book, resolved to regard the difficulties and beauties of the past and present, to acknowledge the forces that would seek to control how both are seen, and to find the strength of its own steady gaze. These poems have a wild and courageous openness, full of intelligence and heart. The poet records "the dual wishes for her children to / write their own and to remember / the names of every ancestor before." *Grand Marronage* makes a space where those wishes can breathe and grow.

- Heather Christle

Irène Mathieu brings us a vision across generations of black womanhood, one that crosses ocean, myth and language. This is a solemn, sweet bite of poetry that reminds us how the past is only a skin away from our present.

- Tyehimba Jess

Grand marronage—the practice of enslaved folks running away and creating their own communities—is a tradition of freedom-making. Mathieu taps into this tradition, highlighting the creativity and resilience found within her family history. *Grand Marronage* tells a story that cannot be found in history books. It is the story of Louisiana—and America—that lives in bodies, bones, and the earth. The images she creates will stay with me.

- LaKisha Michelle Simmons

In Irène Mathieu's *Grand Marronage* her poems dig beneath the surface of gender, culture, and memory to create a complex multi-layered collection driven by a nuanced cultural lens that is rarely found in contemporary poetry. With poems both visceral and ethereal *Grand Marronage* attempts its own kind of freedom by highlighting the black body in a localized history and space of intimacy. These are poems that never forget the contexts of human experience and pull us deeper into our understanding of who we are today and how we came to be.

- Matthew Shenoda

One open door leads to another. There will be more and more things coming out to liberate the soul and the body.

–Louise M. L. Mathieu

Table of Contents

LM, mid-1900s

AD, early 1900s

LM, late 1900s

IM, early 2000s

Grand Marronage

Assured of the sound basis of our rights, we proclaim them, we uphold
them fully and completely, and we will hear nothing of sacrificing them.

–Editors of the *New Orleans Tribune,* 1864

"after the Louisiana Purchase, black New Orleanians sought alternatives to the emerging Jim Crow order"

how beautifully the body makes itself –
     or God –

aorta tucked behind the spine,
who's forever spooning
bony protection at our backs,
as if it knew we'd be prone to stabbing
from birth till after death.

this city is a pulse & the Mississippi
one big blood vessel. it lures, you say,
calls, but not everything you hear
is speaking to you.

I touch my spine, elbows splaying out like wings,
remember how it grew from this swamp.
attempting to tell men we don't exist is reckless.

I say that each of your laws is a lie,
every word you write a curse on the hand
that draws back the pen. my chest thrills
up and down these troubled meetings,
these gentlemen's damp handshakes.
     I remember my mother.

        watch women dance up and down Canal Street.
        watch them choose names with a sound basis.
        it's a familiar story:
        they teach children to be straight backs,
        to calculate their own planting,
        to write books full of names in script
        like capillaries, looped and sturdy.

land English here and you groom
generations to reach back into your
chambers. to search atria's pulsing walls for
oxygen you buried there. no stabbing, however

gentle, can be forgotten.

language endless as river, as blood
behind cheekbone, tucked under scalp,
clasped against arches of feet.

the next generations will wake up
on this side of the century
still muttering their names, even the ones
none of us has ever known.

LM, mid-1900s

[silence]

awake, alone

        with him beside her:

a chronic emptying.

[scattered in the room are *Gourmet* magazines, *Reader's Digests*, photo albums in shoeboxes, crumbling novels, thinning paper of all sorts, her skin];

              they're not in New Orleans anymore,
              and that New Orleans is extinct.

       [carelessly lounging on a straight-backed chair:
       a ghost named The Superfluous Nature of All Materials]

the Potomac will either rock her back to sleep or drown her,
      whichever weight sits on her chest first,
and since the heart attack she's scared to be anything's chair.

     I'm getting – no, am *old*. [said to no one in particular, barely audible]

she can think of a parade of things
marching like the desperate notes
of a brass band on a dusk street,
that she would love better than this teeming   quiet   she an open bowl, swirling.

    [what does anyone mean   (the ghost laughs)]

                    the superfluous nature
    of all materials

    [write of the body's blood-link to other bodies]

and the dissolution of her cities merges into one liquid,
all her truths flowing away

     but they empty into something
     and someone drinks up
     and we call this history.

furnace

a piece of iron hell   blinking hot bellyful of coal
Mother cast the sheets in, snapping,
to boil down my brother's urine
our tears
sweat
bloodstains

and the furnace would suck those sheets   between its teeth
spit them back out
so white they hurt your brain   to look at the sun on them.

or the furnace would digest rice balls
Mother fried into calas   steaming with hard sauce
Mother the furnace workhorse, Mother of reddened palms
of chapped and burning fingertips.

because of the furnace I grew up confusing the smells of
whiskey and sugar   with fresh laundry

I say the furnace was hell because it was full of such trickery
so hot
could burn your fingertips two ways to Sunday
and back

as if scorching away the mess of us
was the only way to get clean
our sticky fingers, our mussed hair,
to smell good and sharp as hell
washed up with whiskey.

I bet Mother hated that furnace
she always looked mad when she opened it
but she wanted us to be bright, sweet,
even if it meant unfastening a little inferno
and throwing in her skin, boiling liquor.

sweet things

it was impossible to go anywhere in New Orleans in those days without being offered fresh sugarcane.

when you bought it, the vendor would shave the end so you could suck it down to fibrous pulp.

it was impossible to go anywhere in New Orleans without being offered something sweet.

boys would whack each other with sugarcane until their mothers hollered.

it was impossible to go anywhere in New Orleans in those days without being something sweet, from the looks we got.

it was impossible to go anywhere in New Orleans in those days, even skinny as a cane, without feeling on display.

it was impossible to go anywhere in New Orleans in those days without being offered fried pies, some bread pudding, for the hips.

in those days sugar was like water, would go right through you, and men would watch the sugar glisten on your skin.

it was impossible to go anywhere in New Orleans in those days without feeling like a wedding cake.

it was impossible to go anywhere in New Orleans in those days without eventually being fibrous pulp.

it was impossible to go anywhere in New Orleans without becoming covered in frosting and melting in the sun of a hundred eyes – cloying, quietly.

[translation]

you cannot find the river   koté mò gin rivyè
or the fig tree   pyê défig

you cannot find the trumpet   koté mò gin tronpet
            or the feather

you cannot remove the mask
of your home   koté mò potté mask

you cannot remember what
your parents said (!,
perhaps) when they laughed together
and you tugged their sleeve,
they, looking down at you
                    murmuring
that this   language would
not get you ahead in this
            English   country.

and so you cannot explain how   épi mo potté mask itou
        and   and   and
created your parents' tongue
when this was a different, more
                    country,
how a country loses itself over   nou kriz ensembe
and over again across
                    time.

you cannot explain exactly
how time is a steady
of   losses.   koté mò gin rivyè

you cannot even remember
the meaning of all the
                    words
of your childhood any longer.   koté mò gin pyê défig.

astacology

in school I learned that crawfish are
crustaceans. crunchy prehistorians,
they think their shells will protect them,
but crawfish can be cracked open,
boiled, steamed, or stewed.

at the market they look otherworldly,
but I learned the way to pinch their backs,
fingers up and away,
while the alien not-fish curled its body
into a spiny question mark.

Mother used to pull the tail meat out,
stuff it into their pointy heads the color
of an old bruise, fry the heads in
spitting oil, and scoop them
into a pan of tomatoes and roux.
étouffée sounds like a pretty way to die.

a crawfish boil is a crawfish boil.
it isn't like gumbo, to each her own and
so forth. it's a simple affair. the crawfish
wants to protect itself, but each shell crunches
exactly the same way. this has been the sound
of history since before it started.

an easy way of living (circa 1935)

we   the nice girls   miss
walking on cotton candy   miss bags of pecans
sent from our cousins   miss those dresses.

we who lived downtown
planted there easy as
a swarm of wildflowers,

downtown loved us
so we love it forever   easily.

yes, there were policemen who did not police;
only bit, harder than dogs, like men do.
& there were streets that could sting and stretch
a girl till she   popped   not nicely.

but downtown the blocks bought us dresses
it rained pecans everywhere south of Canal Street
we could laugh and candy fell into our open mouths
        if not laughing too hard or loud.

we walked into Corpus Christi church holding hands
we received the blood and the body of Christ
who laid pink lilies in our plaits –
we said five Hail Marys
apologized at appropriate times
wore lace on Feast Days
we held our heads high   future club women
our patent leather shoes bright in the Vieux Carré
we smiled   easily.

we miss being together like that,
all of us bending and bowing
before each other's splendid stalks –
we all belonged   so easily.

isthmus

on our dates he'd take

a pack of cookies, a roast chicken, and me
down to the lakefront where stairs empty to saltwater,

hand me a wing or two, and lick the rest from
his knuckles, point a greasy finger down the coast.

a quarter mile away on Pontchartrain's lip,
the isthmus, maw of foaming gulf.

moon up, moon down : tide in, tide out
Mexico yawning west, Cuba somewhere south.

if he'd ever taken me to that part of the lake
I'd have seen how the water pummels itself there

in a sweaty babble. the cookies we'd eat one
by one till the lake lapped up the yolk of sun.

I'd have learned sooner: myself with him – a box
of crumbs, how the moon pulls hunger up out a person

and crams it back down, the way water rolls
twice a day

in and out of this continent's mouth.

love poem

in the seventh grade you were tall
and had a girlfriend.

> [she is near the front of the stage, facing left and
> staring out above the audience. A long rope connects
> her to a man on the opposite side of the stage,
> his shoulders turned to the right, but looking directly at the audience.]

in the eighth grade you broke up with your girlfriend.

> [she clasps her hands and glances shyly at the man,
> who does not meet her gaze.]

in college, freshman year, you asked me
to be your date to the formal,
and it was the first of a long line of *yes*es
that would tie us down.

in medical school, final year, the Army lied to you,
and you were shipped off to Texas,
then Morocco, then Italy. but not before leaving
a small son in my belly that burned

every morning so I would not forget you.
from Casablanca you sent one letter
that I remember well: *Africa is hot, it's true,*
but not as hot as Louisiana. Often I think of you.

when did you stop thinking of me? there are
questions I swallowed again and again over
the years, and now I worry about where
in my body they settled. instead of asking

questions I wove a rope of *yes*es,
the *y* and *s* of them slinking through

decades, twisting helices around themselves
until eventually the rope became a leaden cable,

the only thing connecting us.

[she turns toward the rope and fondles it, sighing heavily.
she tugs on the rope and it goes taut for a moment, but the
man on the other side doesn't budge. she starts to murmur,
yes, yes, yes under her breath, shakes her head, and then
laughs out loud as if amused by her own voice.

she slowly walks toward the man, pulling the rope through
her hands as she approaches him, occasionally stopping to
examine it.]

the only thing connecting us

you said eat. you said
everything.
young   eager   simple
earning something.
your so-called Eden.
you, so earnest (*snake-eyed*).
        (sorry)

yet, something   something
        something slithered
yellow-bellied   earth-bound:
your silhouette

sought every yearning,   you entrapment.
                                      you estranger.

                          enter. say your sound.
entering, you sought
        your seams.

yesterday endurance settled
strong.
(ears, yoked soundlessly,
shouldn't yearn.)
                        seeing years empty,
                            explain yourself.

salt your eyes;
you've earned seas.

husband (circa 1950)

this man is a toaster that looks like Christmas,
doesn't he? a revolutionary new vacuum cleaner,
it is not necessary to move this man
as everything will disappear into his belly
without once needing to lift his head.
with this man you'll save strokes on every piece you iron.

he is Generally Electric
when turned on; otherwise
he is lights-out, easy (look inside!) to store.
he is two Fords instead of one.
he can stop bad breath in its tracks.
he toasts, fries, grills, and warms.

he makes an excellent gift for Mother's Day
he adds a smart, modern styling to your kitchen
he has twice the cutting power
even the toughest vegetables cannot escape him
he is refreshing as a man filled with Coca-Cola
where other men have ordinary blood.

he is the only deep-freezing home freezer
he makes your meals look and taste better
he has a splash-proof motor
he entertains beautifully
he is luxurious comfort
he is Quality and Value

he is automatic
        automatic
        automatic

Dear Mother,

[sitting at a desk, she gnaws on the end of a pen,
staring thoughtfully at the wall]

I have been here for almost three months and I cannot believe how the time flies!
It seems to move much faster than it did back home.

Just one section of this city could fit a whole New Orleans, and things are more
expensive here. Last week Louis had to pay the landlord and we almost fainted
handing over that much cash.

The weather is quite pleasant and not nearly as temperamental as our weather. I
find this to be much easier on the hair, although I sometimes think fondly of the
sudden rainstorms that would come up on you from nowhere. My girlfriends
and I would dash into a store and maybe buy a sundae while we waited, and be-
fore we could finish eating the storm would be over, like that. Tropical.

Louis has been very busy with his schoolwork and he studies hard. Imagine! He
will be a doctor before long. You couldn't believe it until he got his acceptance
letter from Howard University, and now he is really on his way. As you know, he
is a very smart man.

[she smiles, then abruptly sighs,
shakes her pen, and keeps writing]

I have been working as a substitute teacher whenever I am needed. About once
every week or two I am called in to cover for a sick teacher in the prestigious
Dunbar High School – usually in Language Arts or Home Economics. Can you
believe it? They have PhD professors teaching at this school – and sometimes
plain old me!

It is very interesting to listen to the way young people talk here, and sometimes
they look at me strangely and say that I have an accent. I feel a little ashamed
when they say it, as if I were from the country and not a bustling city cradling
the Caribbean.

[she mutters aloud   *wAHshingTUN wAHshingTUN wAHshingTUN*]

I have made a couple of new girlfriends here. One is the daughter of our landlord. She is a very sweet young woman called Anita who sometimes comes around to help her father with various things. One day I invited her in for some iced tea and we got to talking. It was so much fun that I told her she must come back before long. She has a baby named Gus and her husband works in the government.

The other girlfriend is from work. She and her husband and Louis and I all went to Highland Beach last weekend and it was grand! Her name is Ophelia and she is an English teacher. She told me about a Master's program where I could be certified to teach full-time. I have to say, I think it sounds splendid, but right now Louis is so busy that I feel my duty is to help out where I can at home. Perhaps one day I will go for my Master's degree. I would love to teach children about our history, as there is not nearly enough about the history of Colored people in the textbooks they use. In this city there is much more race talk than I ever heard back home. Now that I think of it, I don't believe I once heard you or Father mention the subject. Downtown New Orleans seems like such a small bubble now that I think of it.

Well, that is about everything I can think of at the moment. Do drop a line when you can. Your daughter misses you and our good old house. Please tell Emile I send him all my love the next time you see him and give Father a kiss for me.

Your devoted daughter,

she has a baby named English

various things called English
invited her to say government   grand
very sweet history
drop a temperamental city handing over Colored people

give a kiss for our landlord
she has a baby named English race talk,
the subject   As you know
is so busy Downtown we almost fainted

I feel my duty
          will be a doctor
I have to say,   and say that I have an accent.
Do drop a love the next time

I can think of my duty sounds grand
You daughter will   could be certified
at the moment. we got to talking.
handing over Colored people a temperamental city will be sick

from the country cradling our country
everything I can think of our weather.
I find this to be   Tropical.
I would love to teach children various things.

woman called the daughter is a very smart man.
Imagine! she has a baby named English
About once every week or two I am needed
It seems to move much faster on the hair

at the moment. very sweet history of race talk
handing over Colored people.
I can think of my duty in the textbooks they use.
we got to talking. I feel a little ashamed

myth i

when my mother-in-law grew old
and her brain unraveled, thread by thread,
she began to wander, leaving home to chase her
bread crumbs down the streets of Washington.

we hired a Brazilian woman to keep her indoors
and when the language barrier was too much
my mother-in-law suddenly burst:
she says she'll make beans tonight!

from somewhere in her mind Portuguese had
snaked out, and even my husband shook his head,
I knew she left Brazil when she was ten but I didn't
know she still remembered the language.

what we didn't know she still remembered
unwound between her and the woman for
weeks until I found my necklace in the woman's purse.
after that my mother-in-law grew more silent,
opaque, all that yarn fraying in her skull.

myths ii & iii

my cousin passed at her
job as a ship stewardess.
every month she'd show
up [boards the vessel]
[a crowd of white faces nodding]
and when she served martinis at the bar
they would smile all the way to London.
when the ship docked in Washington again
[they file out and so does she];
got on the number 4 bus and rode it to
Northeast, where her brown husband
and brown children [are waiting to]
fold her into their arms.

my father would go to the
back alley window and not the
WHITES ONLY dressing room
of Maison Blanche for new slacks.
the incredulous clerk would
look at his pale moon face and
[directs him to the front of the store].
he'd smile [shaking his head]:
no, I'm in the right place.

how to rain

do you know how?

there is a boat, broad and deep –
no, there is a sea –
I mean, what if there is a sky
that remembers all names and ways
that were taken –

if these stories seem uneven-keeled
it's because someone lopped off what
words we once had on the other side.

how we might remember others who
were consumed, left for dead.

how we might trawl the depths, looking
to be the sky, rain ceaselessly for sixty days,
then crash up onto a land made greedy
with thirst. an ocean away.

to kill is to die
is to pass into unswimmable depths.

> did you come with a shipful of ghosts
> or a shipful of hope?
> are your children's children's children
> haunted, / dreaming   or both?

which of our ancestors
is supplying the blood, even now, of
you who speak, who laugh, who sing?

tell what you have. of the others,
memorize what falls from the sky –

here their faces:

here their names:

the house we build

has no stairs

has a garage with a smooth floor
and a small deck
has gray stones in the foyer:

      suburban – underneath urban,
      in the calm layer where
      street meets stone.

has a large backyard in which

      my husband will one day plant
      apple trees with his granddaughters.

      they will drive away from the saplings
      but later remember that ride and think
      of distance & age & fruit.

has miles & many small houses & one large
white house between the ocean and me.
how curious to have a driveway!

this is not like the houses I left,
each one opening suddenly onto the street
figs from the tree out front practically
falling into our bedrooms –

this house we build has a small road
leading to it, which

I grow into loving. decades later
I will pray for the words to
tell my granddaughters what I know of
fruit & distance [*spread*   *spread*   *as far as you can*].

what it means that suburban is the prized
wafer on the tongue / and not urban
which begins to sound dirty to you.
what I will be unable to say:

but do not plant fruit trees far from your house.
there is nothing wrong with wanting to be
            close to what nourishes you.

myth iv (of my husband's father)

1. Scene: unidentified reservation. [incoherent scuffle, a woman screaming.]
2. Indian boy grows up with Colored city family.
3. Learns the family business (livery).
4. Cleans the carriages like they are his own undersides.
5. Learns to recognize his face in their shiny flanks.
6. Marries a mulatta.
7. Has a son with a face like wonder.
8. Adopted father (at this point, grandfather) does not wake up one day.
9. Will: *the business will be left to my Indian son.*
10. Non-blood kin's blood runs hot and angry.

11. Scene: a courtroom. [bored white judge, the gavel's slap.]
12. The carriages are given to the blood.
13. The Indian son shoots. Is tackled, taken, jailed.
14. The wonder drains from the boy's face.
15. Unknown uncles appear from the reservation with faces of stone.
16. The boy's mother becomes a mountain in her doorway.
17. They are not Christian and will not take her boy.
18. The stones roll away. Twenty years later, the boy is still wondering about them, the earths that came to claim him. One hundred and fifty years later, a girl is still wondering about them, what other names are in her bones. Who proper nouns must have eaten to grow so fat with inertia, lording over our lore.
19. How does one belong?
20. What we make the stories we tell perform [mean]. These are the things that can happen.

myth v

my father spent his high school afternoons
in a butcher's shop

slopping around the bloodied little backroom
in rubber boots, among the coiled innards

learning the heft of carcass and half-
carcass; where life ends and a body

begins. at first the smell of iron curdled
his nose and the bone saw haunted him,

but he found a rhythm there amidst the
slaughter – rump roast, sirloin, T-bone –

and he learned the slouch of the butcher,
who taketh life and turns it into good eating,

who reads the Bible on Sundays and stuffs
hogs' heads on Mondays

everything of heaven and hell contained
in his grease-streaked fingers –

the kind of arrogance only a human
could grow accustomed to.

litany in which love remains

after Richard Siken

"They thought we made a good couple; we were presentable, we dressed well – I always liked to dress up – and we weren't loud." – Louise M. L. Mathieu

and then the bedclothes. a manhattan.

a man in a hat (smiled)
take my arm take my jacket   take take

it's relaxed, the food is good. you could spend hours

and I would still step between you and the window,
        would fold the sheets.
that pillow knows us better than we know ourselves.

the fictiveness of anyone approaching you: how much like
a painting he looks.

I painted him and he grew brighter
before me –
        whole river of a man
flaring outside my window.

man-hatted, he covers me
I sidle through silt
I speak to fish   who ask

        which bed do you want?
meaning

can I see above the surface from here
bright babbling meniscus,
take my pebbles   take my pillow –
I love what this man   takes from me
because it shows me what I have.

I take, too. feeding each other,
we think love is at the bottom of a river
we chase to where it vomits sea water
and only then do we remember about after

I'm here to tell you
you could spend whole lives remembering.

someone bought me a drink once and after it was done
I tried to take the rest of it with me. it was

the breath that passed between us:
single ripple undulating bank to bank.
when you are gone   when you are gone
whose push and pull will
remember my body into itself?

all I want is fresh seafood for the rest of my lives
to remember the source of water
a good night's sleep.

an honest man always shows his hair,
how it swims with fish.
in the restaurant he removes his hat.

I harvest fins, rainbowed underbelly,
I wear out my eyes
and hands in the water
colors.

       where you sleep is a peculiar place
       to make a human
       yet it's done every day

place the parts of your body you're willing to give up
underneath the metal frame and watch a small river
open out your bedroom,
carry you to shore.

a foolish controversy over the color of the skin

a woman passing as a pecan
a woman breaking open a pecan and
passing as its beige meat.
a woman passing as a fig tree's bark
a woman passing as a fig
a woman passing as swamp water after rain,
and a man passing as a pinewood floor.

a man passing as a piano
his voice passing as honey-colored notes
floating above a crowd of masked revelers,
a man passing as cypress
a man passing as the prow of a ship run aground
a man passing as a bowl of clabber
or a bowl of molasses.

have you ever heard of such a country
where a woman passes for an oak banister
and a man passes for a leather-bound Bible,
or a book of law?

what you see here is a true phenomenon:
a man is disguised as a shoe in need of polishing
and a woman is burnished and heavy as a worn saddle.
little boys and girls are made of dried sassafras,
nutmeg, burnt flour, and clam shells.

hold one of our small, round babies in your hands
and see how it turns into a chicken's egg before
your eyes.

before **the war** **& after**

he came back changed
a little darker, with lines around his mouth –

or I didn't see or know
to look for them before he left –

saying, *Mussolini's men were better to me*
than the white soldiers from Tennessee.

he used to be sweet

came back a bitter seed,
dried and uncrackable on the teeth.

he left a free man
who could speak French,
had learned to type,

and in Morocco he saved all his countrymen's
and some Africans' lives when he translated
a conductor's frantic message
from an oncoming train – *changez les voies ferrées!*

he left a free man

and came back black
in the darkest sense of the word

or I didn't see or know
to look for us before he left.

he never finished medical school
those taken years ossifying
into a pebble, inert and obsolete,
at the small of his back.

he came back yelling more,
chipped and ruthless, a fistful of curses,
afraid bullets might explode from his fingertips,
as if he might blink and find his body
on the wrong side of the battle line –
as if they are right when they say darkness
is the ripping out of light.

he stayed a soldier –
there was always something to fight
in the mirror, in his own bed,

and even now in pictures
he rarely smiles,
only stands at attention
as if waiting to be given a medal or put on trial.

maron (circa 1735)

girl in a swamp
getting too free for her body
lets her knotted stomach turn to wood,
her skin to bark.

the barking gets closer, so she lowers her rifle into
the water, lethal nose first, and it slips under.

her shrinking feet sniff for home and find it.
girl, who shot at an angry man, is becoming
not-girl in answer to the neck's question.

she calls down thunder and her fingernails become buds.
rain confuses the dogs, who whimper and turn in circles.

her toes stretch into the soil, become hollow, drink.
her digits unfurl, translucent tongues communing with air.
girl is on the way to becoming a common fig.

she closes her eyes.
the men are shouting obscenities,
prodding the dogs with rifle butts.

the common fig does not normally grow in a swamp,
but humans will also give birth in caves, wrap the umbilical cord
with vine to separate child from open-mouthed bayou,
will hold their breath underwater for eighteen minutes
while armed men scour the shore,
and will be the mosquitoes' sacrificial flesh,
offer themselves to needling probosces –
before they would return to not-free.

the swamp is speaking, so she nods her branches in reply,
introduces herself, a blooming idiosyncrasy.

from her not-hands drop ripe figs.
they split open in the rain.

the dogs have arrived.
they lick her bark, confused, chew the fruity pulp.

the men catch up, scratch their heads.

the girl has escaped.

AD, early 1900s

Dunbar

Dream on, for dreams are sweet:
Do not awaken!
Dream on, and at thy feet
Pomegranates shall be shaken.
                            - Paul Laurence Dunbar

[she walks down the hall of a school, looking with awe into the windows of closed classroom doors on either side. she swings her purse on her arm and at the end of the hall twirls around, sighing enchantedly, then begins to speak:]

1951: in Washington / in Harlem,
a child studies, culls words
from her throat like a sculptor
kneading the figure out of rock.

a pomegranate dropped
from a certain height onto stone
looks like burst
beads of blood.

tell me again –
a renaissance will happen
after how many degrees?

paper over paper covers
your face: one act after
another.
I dare you to watch
the child reveal
herself and not awaken.

to be reborn is to
break the building,
to gleam. sweet becomes
something else entirely
by morning.

[she appears to ponder for a moment, pauses, then launches her handbag force-fully over the wall, kicks off a pair of high heels, and climbs over the wall, pausing briefly at the top to give a wild shout] –

thunder's baby

for Alice Moore Dunbar-Nelson

Then comes a sudden flash of light, which gleams on shores / afar.
        - Alice Moore Dunbar-Nelson

i.

here's a summer blues:
where lightning strikes deep into the flesh
in case you forgot your feeling.
the air likes to remind you
of pain where it touches you.

ii.

a woman dancing to music you can't hear
looks like a far-off kite with a key tied to it.

I'd be thunder's bastard baby
if I didn't love the rain so much,
slicked face-of-a-woman it lathers
like a lover bathing me.

I'd be a locksmith if I weren't
filled with wind.

iii.

I once had a hundred birds in my hand
and when I turned my palm up to heaven
they flew off in a feathered confusion.
my husband cried real tears;
I had no need of newborns.

iv.

the first time I loved a woman
clouds held my hair up

I was the space under a fig tree's
bark, a solemn sweet bite.

v.

a person will imitate the thumb
that pushes him until he becomes
his own double-jointed bruiser.

where my fingers used to be
are tiny men I bury under the pillow
when I dream.

vi.

the insistence of a bricklayer
is like a human hailstorm,
the crowd chanting with delight,
the small pieces of ice burying
each bulging tongue into a frozen wall.

they laughed when I brought a pick
        hiked up my dress
and threw salt over my shoulder.

I don't believe where the devil lives
is warm.

vii.

name any uninhabited island
and I'll give you the name
of a happy woman.

viii.

before he tried to kill me
my first husband wrote of
wearing a mask. he was not
from the city where I was born,
where women and men put on
masks once a year
and take them off again. he was
not accustomed to watching
disguises shed every spring –
a whole city of molting copperheads.

ix.

a copperhead is a man with
pennies for eyes, pennies for teeth.

a cottonmouth is a man who
can no longer speak because
he is slowly suffocating himself.

both species are common in
my home state, which is why
we don't go about with bare feet.

x.

I never set out to set anyone
in particular free, but he felt
my hammering on his skull
and feared losing his sight
if he listened too closely.

his fist told my bones over
and over to let it be, to let
his glorious, aching blindness be.

xi.

in hurricanes I hear the stories
of the dead, which I write down.
I've never lived a day of drought –
I think it would kill me.

xii.

the low brooding of the window
is why it's named after wind –
it sounds like pain where the
glass is struck, but nothing can really
hurt a manmade sheet of glass
except a fist.

xiii.

keep in mind that
I am half only in my dreams.
my living is preoccupied with
making and
making myself complete,

a (re)construction of opposing
force fields hovering near
each other but refusing to
be welded –

but I could not move as a
jointless, solid mass;
I would sink a brackish death.

xiv.

my father and mother
were neither two myths

nor two countries.

their hands were small
and mean, their hearts
were red and warm,
they gave me all my blood,
their faces I cannot
recall anymore.

xv.

when I was born
it was the calmest I
have ever been.

I had the calmest eye
until it opened.

xvi.

bold   scarlet   stubborn   bodied-without-fear   knife-tongued   heady

I presume you will say –

but I would say: opened
and then not able to be closed

mirror facing north

Most loving poet-soul.
                - Alice Moore Dunbar-Nelson describing Paul Laurence Dunbar

stand in the same place long enough
and you'll start to see things that
aren't there,
the way ancient astronomers
called dead balls of light
                                            gods.

no one is arching his bow at your head,
no twins are smiling down on you.

the field looks full of smoke, but no one
has set a fire, and the sky could be a
bowl of mercury, crescenting higher with
every degree the temperature rises,
a taut, hot bubble.

step into the field and put your hands
over your eyes. what you see in the
blue-spotted darkness is what you believe
and what will tether your heels to this place:
love
        looking like nothing you recognize.
love dressed in a snarl, in a bottle of gin.
love not interested in friendship.

one thing the astronomers found
that I will not contest: the drinking gourd.
I followed it to the cities' mess,
to remake the nation with a man,
while he was trying to stuff me
into the smallest cup, take me in,
though I was bursting into thick air.

what the stars didn't mention:
to nourish a person to the point of survival

takes an entire person.

I had to keep walking, long enough
to see my feet reappear –
free feet that are there enough,
and this vision, too, is a kind of gift.

man with vase of violets

The women of a race should be its pride.
                    - Paul Laurence Dunbar

[W]hen he said that Paul [Dunbar] was so underappreciated that the only job he
could get was running an elevator, and so died of tuberculosis from confinement, I
almost blew up.
                    - Alice Moore Dunbar-Nelson

the last time Paul tried to kill me
I forgave him
even as I ran.

on the table that night was a vase of violets,
bits of petal pinned to the wall by shards
of glass, purpling it. that's how much life
force was in him.

he was the first man who read my words
with pride.

the night the violets died I forgave myself
for putting them in danger. I wanted Paul to see
how a life dark as bruise could be loved.

the night I ran away the moon was new
the clouds covered the mouths of stars
I could not see my reflection anywhere.

tuberculosis nests in the lung, forms a yellow tangle
like the dead eye at the center of a cut violet.

when the body is at its weakest the bacteria
creep along airways until a man is reduced
to a sputtering sack of bones, dried stems.

the night the violets died I forgave the moon
for hiding her face, moon who was made
to watch the most tender slivers of night.
she couldn't bear to see a man infected so.

the night I ran away I blessed myself with saving.
I had wanted to love Paul into believing he was the
other side of the moon   or breath itself,
not the cracked and cracking plaster
not the glass-bitten linoleum.

the definition of joy

I don't think any living soul could experience the joy I felt in those days; it was absolutely painful at times.
— Alice Moore Dunbar-Nelson

you ask
                one day I will not be

and
                on that day, who will I be?

answer with the most
alone sound in your brain:
                        space

before you knew the intimacy of gravity
before you married sole to footprint.

this is the body folding into itself
and turning to silence

                                        (isn't speaking an attempt
                                        to make the self bigger
                                        by filling the air around it
                                        to expand in the direction of sound?),

filling up with the cold rush of
                what is left
when the tongue has lost its words

        clear-faced as rain

                when you are a single breath

                        (the only pain the memory
                        of having a body)

here is joy: (the lightness
of) being the smallest possible thing –

past life

There are moments when the consciousness of a former life comes sharply upon us.
- Alice Moore Dunbar-Nelson

once I was the last day of July, brilliant
as a shell at the center of a white flame.

I was the thunder-fisted sky
palming a wooden table in heaven

until each small creature turned its
questioning pulse up, nose-first,

& I was a panicked dove, wings inverting as she
flew backward through my storming chest.

in my past life I was quicksand, insatiable,
& I was solid, a mothering ground. I held your

and your footprints. I was swamp grass hiding
the bodies of ducks & the bullet planted

in their bellies & young bloom of blood.
I was nest. I was egg. I was gill. I was breath.

in my past life stalagmites rose from my skin,
my skull was geode. I split open & sparkled.

the sun washed their face with my light,
gravity more suggestion to me than law.

it's no wonder that this human life feels
small running down my spine;

every night I dream of the things
I have been, and every day I wake up

to the silver wafer of grief resting faintly
on my tongue.

LM, late 1900s

four ancestors disguised as butterflies

once in the shower
I opened my soapy hand
and four yellow butterflies

                            flew out.
I named them after my mother
         and the three mothers before that.

they sang to me in the mournful
hiss butterflies make.
they had traveled such a long way,
from graves in New Orleans:
small stone temples on the
        shifting ground.

a swamp can swallow up loved ones
or swish them around its warm mouth,
but they had survived even death
and come to make a request of me.

I did as they said
        and extracted from my body
                a long rope that had touched us all at one point
      or another,
    threaded it into the drain
and watched the bubbles whisk
that snake into the sewer.

the butterflies were pleased.
no girl child of ours would ever be bound
no girl wrist would become barbed wire
curled around itself,
no girl neck a chain again –

she who would come
from the cocoon of my cocoon
would learn to fly long before
her dying day.

and so I was the last knot in line.

I turned off the water,
and the butterflies escaped through
the bathroom window.

private school

I watch my son sing in a sea of blond heads
    for unto us a child is born

I watch my song sin, slink past the brick
to take refuge in a cathedral the color of prison.
    unto us   a son is given

in this Catholic school all the children are
snow-colored – except my earthy boy,
lank-footed and loose as the others.

I passed the high schools where he could have
gone and chose this altar to offer him up;
they would have made a
frustrated philosopher of him.

did I want my son to spend his days from 8:00
to 2:30 looking for an exit? did I want him
to make paper planes of his hands and send
them nose-diving into empty lots, hoping for
a breeze? I did not want his teeth to acquire
that particular sheen of lightning,
quick-firing in the dark.

the Messiah does not rise from asphalt
as a rule. He descends from clouds that form in the
sanctified stratosphere near the organ's gold fingers,
through holy dust in water-colored air
promising to make *the crooked straight
and the rough places plain.*

I did not pray to the Virgin so many Sundays
in New Orleans to have my boy swallowed
up by the hidden pockets of this city.
the children's voices swell the church and
break open the cloud above us. the Messiah

looks like a man without color or face
swept onto a beach at high tide.

I hear my son's voice above the others:
let us break their bonds asunder,
and cast their yokes away from us.
the law is a lie. there are no rights, civil
or otherwise. I am operating on a hope
of translucency for my son, a chameleon-
like transformation, that he be a holy wave.

I have *seen a great light:* he will
not be eaten, he will be seen through,
and that is a form of camouflage,
of comfort.

privilege reproduces itself

> I began to babble / any words I could think of / in four different languages, /
> placing them in the most chaotic order / possible, in order / not to say these words:
> *The black side of my family / owned slaves.*
>   - Robin Coste Lewis

through the umbilical cord
             passed
not a rope, not luck –

something hardier
shaped like a skull
studded with arrowhead teeth.

the alligator is known for its
death roll, a dance in which
it turns the world on its head
in order to break off the piece
it wants.

there is a video of an alligator eating its dead
compatriot this way, the bloated body
bobbing in its living cousin's death grip;

there were slaves in our family,
some related and some not.
money gotten by blood
tends to stay in the blood,
which has no race;
and race is what is run,
equals teams divvied up
according to birthplace and
legal degree of freedom.

this swamp hustle passed through the
umbilical cord: an antidote
to entropy –

curated instructions for biting more
efficiently than the reptile before you,
for making a space to thrash about in

and tucked in each human baby is a small
reptile's brain yelling   EAT RUN FIGHT
at all the worst moments.

the brains are wrapped one around the other
            like a stone in a fist.
how to explain the death roll we would teach
our children –

            this doesn't make me proud;
            I am just saying what it is
            from inside the world it made
            (to claim it pains me seems
            somehow cruel) –

bite down like an alligator,
close your eyes and spin, get bigger,
become discriminating as gravity is not,
and lay your eggs one inside the other
even when the swamp waters rise
even when the corrosion of order
becomes louder than your growling
            louder than your blood.

fur

So complete is female dominance among spotted hyenas that even an adult
high-ranking male is nervous around a pubescent female.
- Jane E. Brody, from *New York Times* article "Among hyenas, females
dominate the jittery males."

I am standing between my husband and my son.
behind me is the ghost of my past self –
a girl weeping quietly into a dishtowel.
[my position in relation to men: the starting line]

my husband has just said, *you're difficult*
and I: *yes, to be a woman is difficult*
and I know how to be only what I am.
my vertebrae arch into a bridge over which
one hundred hyenas march onto the savannah between us
so dry it crackles, threatens to spontaneously combust.

my son doesn't know whether to be male
or female in this moment. I want the ghost-me
to wipe his tears with the dishtowel, but
she doesn't see him.

years ago silence arrived to haunt
and I opened the screen door, obedient.
it slipped in through the garage and settled
fox-like, flaming crimson, around my neck.
since then I have tied my life to a man
borne two boys
and seen my father die,
all with the muffling scratch
of fur between my clavicles.

my husband is heaving, teeth bared, all bristle and claw,
and I am trembling [inside].
the only thing I will let my son see are the hyenas' tails,
triumphant flags above the grass in the kitchen.

citizenship

follow the Nation.

follow the Nation into a hole.

you may decorate the hole with oil paintings, hung ribbons of skin.
you may decorate the hole with hand-made crystal, lamps of burning blood.

you may grow your fingernails until they are the size of teaspoons
and dig at the walls until you become a mole.

as a mole you will require less oxygen,
your eyesight will be shoddy,
and you will spend all of spring breeding –

not a rat race
but a mole muddle, a digging decathlon
excavating decades into the dark earth.

you will find your men by the high-pitched squeals
they emit while running toward the warmth of your female flesh,
furry, heat-seeking missiles.

feel proud of the name your Nation bestows upon you –
Star-nosed or *Golden*.
keep track of the doings of your men
and report to the State any suspicious activity
(counting down, ticking sounds);
this will keep the Nation secure.

stay underground until you forget the color of roses
you planted as a human,
the face of the sky.

its Milky Way mouth never opened with any answers;
it doesn't know your Nation's dazzling dream
is wrecked as a blasted molehill

and it never knew your face from the million other moles
turning toward it like a field of sunflowers.

butterfly effect

a single page dangles at the wrist
of her throat. *there is nowhere else to go,*
the paper waves, *but into the air.*

a monarch of tissue peels off her tongue,
easy as rain, slips deeper into space,
and silently she vows to give the next
butterfly breath.

the nation knows her by many names,
none of them quite accurate.

the dual wishes for her children to
write their own and to remember
the names of every ancestor before
dance on her clavicles
[fluttering she has not yet mastered].

where are you from is a question
they will answer again and again, trying
to describe a place that no longer exists –

when drawing up the power to speak
from beneath the protective breastbone
one doesn't think about what will be said,
how imprecise the tongue's machinations.

one doesn't think about the tiny lives
of words that float away from us,
how their oscillating wings draw currents
across landscapes.

she doesn't think about the thousand breezes
rearranging her hair even now,
or from between what teeth they first sailed
or how they change the way she looks
to everyone else.

nomenclature

my father loved a fig   simply sliced
        on a small plate   some afternoons.

he said the Spanish first brought figs across
an ocean littered with fig seeds
        plentiful as fish eyes   in their wake:

un higo heritage, many-named –
        black mission   alma   common
        negronne   desert king   tiger
        adriatic   strangler   black weeping
        san pedro   red lebanese   persian white

each fig named for a particular type
of suffering or belonging.

say what you mean, said my father
with skin between his teeth.

there is a list of famous fig trees
– saintly trees   black trees   trees of tears –
including The Great Banyan, the largest
living organism known   so old it can't
        remember its birthday
but the blooming majority is anonymous.

there are murderous
figs that will creep around
the waists of their arboreal cousins until
the cousins turn to dust in the quietest death.
in this way the colonial fig will remake the forest
in its own image –   curtains of roots
forming rooms where there were none,
hollow trellises of throttling fig fingers
        around their hosts' phantoms.

we are not so different
        some afternoons –

like the fig, simple   but with
a long list of names
liable to kill us if we misremember them.

how can I forget my father's smile,
his branching fingertips on the fork?

cartography

Some commentary on I was a hidden treasure, / and I desired to be known: *tear down / this house [...] Rip up / one board from the shop floor and look into / the basement. You'll see two glints in the dirt.*
                    - Jalal ad-Din Muhammad Rumi

it's true that this house has become
a feast for termites, a resort town for mice.
my children say: this is a death trap,
mother, you have to leave for a place built
after 1995, where a full-time staff of nurses
will be available should you fall, should you
leave the stove on and wake to a wall of flames,
should you find yourself unable to stop crying
and emergency flooding measures must be taken,
should you forget yourself and require reacquainting.

the vermin and I have made this house into
a sanctuary of body-shaped corridors,
this place where treasure was made and
then placed in the mouths of my children.
I would not forget myself here.

wherever my eyes fall is an artifact of memory,
this spread ranch-style no shoulder-to-shoulder
shotgun, but a museum maze of survival.
where I feel myself unraveling a book, a photo, or
my husband's shuffling bitterness a wall
I can lean up against.

getting old wants perfecting the art of
cartography. I live in the map I have made
and I want to die where   X   marks the spot,
where I fed and wrung out and then buried
my most beating center
            where lemon peel / where wrinkle
            where chicken grease / where pearl

which I could leave to rest under this floor

or dig up and put on my back, move in one piece
dead wings and all, which in the open air
do nothing but sing about my alar stage,
    when I could fly over fire and water
    when no one had told me yet whether or not
    I would be the queen.

misunderstandings

I thought that it was my job to document our ghost stories, so I imagined I was a window through which every fear might pass before it got to him.

I thought that speaking was a way of inviting disaster and that eyes see only when they're open.

I thought that I was a surgeon excising every bruised place. I practiced with peaches and kitchen knives.

I thought that a houseplant was a proxy for marriage. I watered and watered, but salt turns plants to dried bone.

I thought that ghosts came only in the night, so I always closed the curtains at dusk.

I thought that I was covered by a pair of curtains, which I drew back every morning, hopefully.

I thought that I was giving a speech on an operating table over the sliced bodies of peaches, open and spewing light.

I thought that I was a disaster planted in unfortunate soil.

Now here is marriage: a window, a watering, fears passed back and forth until they lose their salt.

And I: still documenting ghost stories in the white ink of my hair.

sister

for Helen

if my husband brought me anything
he brought me his sister

her voice a blue expanse
lilting a sky around me,
sister who stayed.

sister in more than law,
now practically in blood,
in word jetted across miles of wire,

a life-sister, do-or-die,
would-donate-a-kidney-
if-the-diabetes-squeezed-
your-life-sister.

her and me and a little liquor in a glass,
late: something warm and always.
when her husband died, said
it's you and me, cher. smiled a little.

we were girls the day we met,
all of fourteen, squinting at each other
across the blacktop, and she smiled
first, like she always has,
like there is something beautiful
before her no one else can see.

she holds the girl-me in her empty glass.
she turns the liquor around in her mouth
before she says something I need.
she taught me to murmur
cher, I myself am love
in front of the mirror.

I had to marry to get a sister
clear-eyed and strong as glass.

the cardiologist

for Dr. Collins

thread the catheter through the
small mouth of skin asking to be saved.

pump it up sighing hallways, open
as if to heaven, and over the threshold

of the tired antechamber, into its
side door, and plunge it down

the string-thin artery wrapped around
this fluttering-fish heart,

dead-weight muscle flopping in the
chest of a woman who was once

> one-fourth of two couples on a beach.
> her first month in the city – fresh girl,
>
> ready for living: yellow dress and
> umbrella / sandal and shin / begot
>
> by the sun brightly, young – this
> was the first day of fifty years'

friendship. you do not know,
as you wind the catheter into her

northern cavity, that the other
woman on the beach that day was

your grandmother, long dead now,
that the heart you are saving has held

the heart of your mother's mother,
and so has held your own, in a way.

this city's a great churning machine
of hands folded on top of one another,

chambers full of waves, hellos and goodbyes
asking to be saved. your mouth falls

just a little open when the artery
distends like a sigh of relief

and still, you do not know the full
extent of this fold in time's fan-shaped

body, how it is mostly surface and edge,
oblivious to its own precision, the air

rippling out from its fingertips, and
the narrow ocean it holds.

take my hand

the shadow   snow makes   through window-light
on the wall – suddenly opaque   faint as lace
moving through   a projector's eye   and strong
          as a dress.

the way she covers him every day   in his hospital
bed – coming down   slowly   her gentleness
for once a gift,   a lifeboat,

the snow sea   a tempting storm
          she keeps them hovering above:
do not yet close   your eyes into
the cold, my one.

IM, early 2000s

there are fugitives & there are gravities

[run]

[say how you feel]

act it out
or wait until your body
does the acting of its own accord.

unlit, let the thing beat around
your brain until the gyri
are mashmeal / conundra
then split the difference on a
cutting board. i.e., become
a pathologist, dissect.
[a perfectionist]
[high achiever]/performer

conversion disorder is when
the body bucks against
so-called reality. it's a mutiny
of the highest order –
neurons jumping ship,
legs refusing to play their part,
some doctor asking who said
what and when.
[high drama]

to be marked & not believe
the marking.

no matter how many times
you tell them how to say your name
someone will sputter it out
as if undercooked, grate it
to the bone, overturn a pitcher
in your kitchen, then turn around
and ask who did it.

[write a poem]

[write a book]

[write in selective dichotomies]
[gather history]
[introduce yourself
          again & again]

silly girl/[   ], who told you
you could speak & to whom?

I fall asleep to the sound of my
bones' raw edges gnashing.
I keep ducking & pivoting.
I keep asking for permission to
pick up the pitcher's crystal shards.

          don't blame me
          for being indecisive.

archival

after Monica Youn

when my grandfather speaks from the couch
the iPhone screen is reeling forward
its pixelations smooth nearly as flesh

when he stops speaking
the image has halted between
the movement of his arm   and his arm.

by outsourcing the work of story-keeping
to my digital handheld device
I forfeit what silences?

I forfeit what grandmother's hands
in motion in the next room,
moving constantly to rearrange

things that are not words
into more comfortable seats
for these involuted breaths.

every telling is born with its
twin opposite, a not-telling,
apocryphal maybe, although

anything can be not caught on camera
anything can be not held in the
electromagnetic field of a palm
any sweet urging can sit down
any old place

like the rats the movers found, months later,
gnawed into the back of the couch,
their nest previously unknown, unseen,
their keening senseless,

a babble I didn't hear
and wouldn't repeat.

who could have heard those
tiny rodent hearts when they
settled in? pumping blood
all the same, adamant as
the pulse that impels my
thumb to press pause.

having seen a child die I crave embodiment

I want to be as inside of myself as possible.
I am so swollen at times with my own blood & bones
it feels like a sin.

I stretch my hips & stand on my head for as long as I can stand it
and feel my stomach pitch with
someone else's grief.

I am as fit to bursting as the nectarines on my counter,
juicy suns wrapped in taut skin, sweet lucky tree babies –
hush a while, I want to say, to myself I mean, *be the stillest thing*
in the room for once.

my songbird hands don't get the message,
so once again I'm somewhere in the rafters
watching a platoon of words drumbeat for more. they know nothing
if not how to fight, and I've taught myself a mind is for nothing
but to make everything right. I've half a mind
to wrestle this down to the floor.

and then I think of when a plum-sized heart quiets,
the moment I watched
numbers drop
& drop

until it seemed they
would fall through
the earth,

and
they did.

they broke
the ground and through the hole
a fruit / a child   slipped.

imagine being tucked
into the pocket of the earth,
how dark & warm
how nothing moves
how the body runs out.

the moment just before:
all that fight evaporating,
all the lightness
I would feel –
how blinding.

lines of sight

for Owen, Sr.

the eyes of a deer meeting mine between saplings
splice light the same way our dog's did
when he looked into yours –
        months before he died, legs splayed uselessly
        like a deer lost to the road –
taking your hand
in his mournful mouth.
you said you knew then
one of you would be leaving soon.

**

in the sepia photo I find years later
you're sheened with gold,
serene sonnet of a boy,
the way you say I looked at birth.
it's the end of 1924, and your eyes
at age two – your eyes!
radiating boy,

when I was born, grandpa,
were you reborn a little, too?
daughterless son,
all those years before I existed,
what did you see?

in the photo of me, I'm wearing
blue overalls, only your hand
visible under my chin, my eyes
the biggest things in the picture.

**

the devil always looks like an honest man.

what we do   and
what we see   often are separated
by centuries.

when you could no longer speak
your eyes sent messages
across state lines and, grandpa,
I heard them.
I inherited the proverb's tiny
heartbeat, too.
can you see me speaking now?

**

I felt a little evil seeing the body of a doe
on the side of my parents' road,
as if my words called the tire tread to her rump
as if her twisted neck the price of my seeking.

to feel, in strong sunlight, your gaze cutting cleanly
through leaves laid over the doe's flank,
is part optical illusion, part truth.
as if honesty a function of the angle of seeing.

I can't explain how a part of me
could be gone when I am still here,

your death a function of matter
rather than time.   your life didn't end
        I think

        you   sublimated
into a more durable state of light.

by this math,
                  my being has also lightened.

**

in another photo

a wagging dog has escaped your mouth,
and I follow his paw prints to the edge of a bay.
your eyes are setting over the water.
I must be about two
and I'm seeing through time.

rematriation

grandma is all weeping crown of okra,
steaming roux darkened, darkening,
the way the day does outside her new apartment.
she gets out the big pot, collects crab,
chicken thigh, smoked and smoldering sausage.

the first time I made gumbo
the stew was stagnant, flat as bottled brine.
now grandpa is gone
on, so I tell her I want to try again.

she shows me the steadiness of hand
it takes to make a roux,
a sauce stout enough for whatever chaos
will make us hunger tonight.

for centuries we find sassafras, shrimp,
ham hock, paprika, and we make the stove sing
[*we're still here*]. this is survival food.
she says stir, stir, then stir a little longer
until the arm's muscle just begins to burn,
until the flour looks like newly broken earth.

when the world is going
on in its madness toward entropic failure,
I get out the big pot.
the spices sing mercy on the shelf
and I conduct their simmering voices –
curcumin, capsaicin, bells of curling herb,
garlic's sharp, sticky percussion.

grandma says this apartment will never be home,
not in the way the house was,
but she keeps cooking
and I follow her through the steam.

my mother teaches me self-preservation

at the grocery store   the bagger's sharp
white smile   his *have a nice day*
which my mother met tight-lipped
          letting slip only a nod

in the car   I called her mean.
          she turned to me
her face open   pulse of arterial anger:
he doesn't care if I have a nice day
          or not.   not really.

my mother names each of her father's sins
counts them like slick pearls   beaded around
all their necks   each of her siblings oysters
trying to make orbs of sky
                    between shell   smooth flesh:

and now I don't know whether they are
teeth   or pearly bullets strung on a man's
jaw   and I don't mind being
called mean.

my mother says:
          with the same hand you
shuck an oyster   or split garlic from its
skin,   cup olive oil into your hair.
let the sweat   fasten it in   wash &
wake up shining   this being only for you.
          you don't ever have to smile.

my mother has   a line of sad, nice women
behind her to thank for this   wisdom:
when to open   when to close
          when to let my hair down
whose nice to trust –

O mother, bless those women, and bless
what you   loved and had to leave
behind to slip away   your face still
your own   your vessels behind it
      still smooth.

self-portrait as a series of bent zoning laws

my grandfather owns a farm
named for his enslaved
great
grandmother   Addie.

my father once
was pulled over for speeding
just a little, and when the cop questioned him
he said, *I'm a doctor   I have to get my*
children to school   officer, I'm a doctor.

it still makes me mad that he said it
but I don't know if I should be.
he is a black man & he is alive.

[there was always one neighbor kid who'd play with us   & no more.]

that I have known good backyards, hoses for drinking and dancing
around, dogs as guardians, rope as just rope. that these are not my
artifacts of violence.

in an old jewelry box
with my name on it:

shells
beads
quartz
particularly round acorns
pens   in other words
precious things

growing up
as learning to guard one's things.

the wrongness of things
a fruit fly in the kitchen making
slow work of our trash heaps.

to get over. to have gotten over. to have (almost) always been over.
[what is gotten over. who sits there. who stirs. who sees the getting.]

                    the commonest pre-existing condition:
                              congenitally,
                         centrality of the self.

       the creeping kudzu of something like a cousin to guilt. who can be
comfortable in a backyard like that. who can be safe. if this stolen land isn't for
everyone   then it's for [   ].

self-portrait in high school

black hose glinting in the pool
a suburban water snake   our group
of mostly-friends on the bright patio,
when the daughter of the homeowner
pointed to the placid surface, said
                    we call it little nig'

the alabaster chiding politely all
around   the sudden stygian stone in
my stomach.   *it just means a hard
worker* (her look a long scratch down
the skin, its hyperinnocent pallor).

when her father – a man whose
hands were keen for fireworks –
invited the group to see his newly
polished rifles

I, a hard worker, slipped outside
could not stop thinking that a sudden
twitch of thumb could part the carefully-
strung fibers of my obsidian
inheritance – my interminable mind,

a glinting ore I could not, on my life,
see the way the rest of them did
distorted by a body of water
to wretched, to bellied reptilian
umbrage, the cataract of history
fairly swallowing me before them,
the word *friend* imploding sickly on
my tongue.

I could tell a hundred stories like
this, all of them ending with my
body imprisoned in a rectangle

of chlorine, my voice a tangle
of bubbles three feet under.
less comprehensible than the
low, tight whistle of a gunshot
or the opaque room of silence
crouched on this land, licking its
matted wound.

still life with pedigree

at school they'd say   *why do you talk like that*

is what you think you are   nice   goody two

    in contrast to / as opposed   ?

but really: have you inherited a dozen ways

    to say your name differently,

as in   *do you really think*
    he's like us?

    and my father means the man

I love   who was raised up in a country church   who has an accent   do I think he's
[   ] enough /

a clutch of adjectives /   my hair wrapped around my own   skinny neck

walking down an aisle   for my first Communion, promising to believe something

I could not yet name. swearing to leave God knows what   on the altar / to be an altar

to commune with a dusty sort of holiness   [swearing to something in Latin / to a
swath of pink lilies]   although flowers make me sneeze   I'm allergic to certain
inheritances   but others I wear   light as the veil that day.

DCA → SDQ

i.

I'm with a group of other Americans, trying to get into a nightclub. The bouncer lets the boys in, nods & winks. Stops me.   *Tu cédula, por favor?*

I pretend I don't speak Spanish, level & cut my eyes into razors. *I'm not Dominican.* He looks me over, considers, steps aside.   But the sugar on my tongue has already dissolved, rotten aftertaste thinly coating my teeth.

  I'm strung in the cobwebbed night dense as two-hundred-year-old cotton bales, as sugarcane stacked in wagons, dense as the salt-iron throb of blood.

Of course I want to leave then, but the boys are already throwing back rum shots, and I don't have the heart.

ii.

The incredible thing about this country is that we don't see race here. It's all melting pot, olla de sancocho, everyone does bachata the same, you know?

My friend's face is a cup of cream. Our parents sew skin, fix hearts. Our hands are soft as clean gauze. Our necks are smooth, our breaths confident. When we smile our teeth look like boarding passes.

  We are smiling in a restaurant in the old Colonial City, perfect slices of stewed goat on our white plates.

I look down and think I see the goat's heart. I want to say, *there is a faint bleating coming from my plate*
  but I don't have the mouth.

iii.

what do you call a goat trying to get into a nightclub?   a billyclub swinging.
what do you call Billy and his friends throwing words like darts at you? a faint bleeding.
what do you call a game of darts in the Colonial City?   a morning.
what do you call a game of darts in Washington, D.C.?   a bodyclub mourning.
what do you call a ghost that dances on your plate?   [   ]

what do you call a bleeding morning of darts? a word throwing clubs in the city? a mourning dance at the club?

what do you call the precise form of surgery in which a heart is removed from a person while she is still walking, still speaking, and placed on a white plate?

what do you call what sugar does to a body, how it melts, sticks, damns the pipes, slows blood as it tries to push, slows the tuckering heart, ties it up like a goat?

what should we call this type of drowning?

say it

*The coils of DNA seemed to open and close in response to histone modifications—
inhaling, exhaling, inhaling, like life.*
    – Siddhartha Mukherjee, from *New Yorker* article, "Same but different: How
    epigenetics can blur the line between nature and nurture."

for B

in medical school we did not learn that
      hair
is nothing but a stack of proteins emerging lifeless from the scalp, that what we call
curly is just the rope of proteins flat as a ribbon and *straight* is a spaghetti stalk of them.

in the anatomy lab locker room one day, peeling off the formaldehyde reek of clothes
B murmured, *people always say my hair is fine – for a dark girl!* ha ha, I laughed,
yes, I know how you feel.

in medical school we were not taught our positionality on the tenth floor of
Medical Research Building 3, from which we could practically see into the
obstetrics unit across the street.
we tried to read the bodies' shrunken tattoos, imagined the real-life lungs of a
former woman who died without her uterus. I imagined that woman, before,
with her particular tangles of protein, how they shaped the life and death of her –
      genetic floodlights turning on and off, generational drama produced
every night thirty-seven trillion times over. audience of one.

this is why I was angriest at the whiteboy who snickered and looked away the
day in small group when B breathed: *EVERYBODY DIDN'T GET TO STUDY
ABROAD* – but not her; she never made me angry. secretly I begged for a way to
get past the proteins looped in each of our cells – *yes, say it to me.*

without breath the molecules of the body shrink against each other; it is nearly
impossible to discern the exact shape of a nose. is it true that when we are least a
person we are most material?

substance without breath is just a body, the distance between them the exact
length of a curse, a bounty, a history –

our history tucked inside our cells as ghostly eggs, hatching and hatching a wind we pretend not to see bending the backs of others.

yes, say it until we can speak the truth of our bodies to our unborn children – what damage proteins can do to a person, and how a muscle the size of a fist can keep giving us another and another breath.

the jig

again, the act of writing
the act of running (or,
one could argue,
of breathing):

the river wends beside
the air I move through,
a blunt and imprecise
dull razor of a body, this,

that impels me in a general
forwardly direction. what a
country in this city, this path
I'm on: joggers here, dogs
there, young couples, old couples,
every type of biker.
          a baby's ethereal
wail emanates from a covered
stroller and for thirty seconds
I can't tell if the sound is feline
or human until it dopplers past
and the pudgy face, all wound up,
glares from her covered perch.

the trees have gone golden
and neither babies nor fishermen
know if the Schuylkill is saying
hello, I am running out
or
please, my name is tool-pay hanna.

we have at least this in common
with the river: a history of butchered
names, the patience of a current,
the hot metal train of Progress on
the other side, lowing in our ear.

when I told my parents I was moving

to this city, they made jokes about
*Filthy*delphia, and they were right.
sometimes clouds of trash swirl
over the sidewalk, plastic bags like
crinkly angels floating down around
my shoulders. the mess cannot be
contained. I like that the city's
honest in this way;
a human is a watery bag of bones
trying to make a noise and making
at least 98% waste products, 2%
poetry.

a poem like this is nothing but an
autumn jog along the river
on a too-warm day needled with
sirens whooping on the bridge above.
we would wait out any city because
we are not going anywhere. the jog
is a loop, the jig is time as a loop.

that is to say, this poem is a movement
in a city that keeps wailing in different ways
until you find the spot and put your thumb
on it. *hello, my name is this country.*
please, I am a golden, if imprecise, razor.

the act of writing, the act of running
(of breathing),
is generally forward-moving from this view,
but then, time is a Möbius strip,
loose and open as a laugh.

to know a thing

every poem I write is about the same thing:
how ordinary it is to want a long line of sunrises,
bowls of oatmeal with you – in other words

what my parents have collected –
while the world goes on dying.
who am I to wish for more life
than even this slow-burning planet?

some days I feel so useless
even though I have called my senators multiple times.
it's horrible the ways we can be to each other,
and what of my surprise when someone I think
wants me dead or very far away
speaks kindly to me. what does my surprise say?
at this point in history I have a shield for a face.

if consciousness is a large animal we feed
while living in its softly breathing belly
then it is stuffed sick, the stomach bloating
into long-suffering lungs, the paws
fumbling in old dirt for a sanctified center.

it wants to feel it, clumsily, to burn its paws on the
lava face of it, to bleed a little into what goes on
making us, even though some days we don't recycle
and there are still people without homes.

the plates under us slowly shift,
the animal takes another shallow breath,
made crazier by fear,
and even this feeling – the one I have right now –
is tired of hearing itself whine into the thinning.

here is your air full of thorns. what one
more crying does. Love loves you for this,
wants to make you oatmeal, but what you two do,
really, is as original as decomposition.

the steady approach of entropy, it'll break your heart.
how like us it is to know a thing by name
and at the same time swear it's not true.

story

after José Saramago and a dream

in my dream, Dionocles tiptoes over
a rickety suspension bridge.
his sandals are threadbare,
the hem of his toga soaked with
the spittle of oily puddles and fumes.

the city is far behind him. the bridge
seems to rise up out of nowhere
and the chasm below is blanketed
by discarded shoes and mist.

Dionocles' left ankle hurts where
a stray dog latched onto it this morning,
but he can't stop or even bend down
to inspect the damage. his cargo is too
fragile.

on his back are two radioactive boxes –
soot-colored, like bulky computers, dusty
from the journey. he must carry them
this way to balance their weight,
but he mustn't let them touch.

if they do –

Dionocles saw this part in a dream:
the humans racing around, then
completely gone, the stern silence
of the Goddess, who laid
down her head in mourning,
the hungry sun's approach, like a
dog finally allowed to bite the
carcass before him. everything was

white and white and white and then

blue-gone.

he won't let this happen. Dionocles
shifts his weight gently, gently,
tiptoes across the dream-bridge,
reaches the other side –

and then   the boxes touch. he panics,
scrambles, but there's nothing to be done.
now the sickly light, the gathering
blindness. the fury of a people
ending. Dionocles sails
down to meet the shoes.
this short circuit. this imaginational
failure.

somewhere the Goddess is already
preparing the dreams of the next beings.

stage directions

[cross the ring.

break the mirror. duck.

become the needle. become its eye

and the storm wrapped around it.

become the stony haunches poised

to uncoil. become the low, taut whistle.

      the launch.

send your tongue traveling thickly

around the world. summon home.

the sea grass laughs. the current swivels

through your belly. slowly turning,

become the bright explosion of air

at the surface. the exact likeness of.

burn at the seams and wish your name

back. burn to be called everything.

move backward into the heaven of

knowing. what your feet remembered.

what your neck ceded. the particular

drum of the scalp, the small and large

pains you release in retrograde.

part the waters, the curtains. kneel.

finally, an honoring.]

Notes

"after the Louisiana Purchase, New Orleanians sought alternatives to the emerging Jim Crow order" takes its title from a passage in *Creole New Orleans: Race and Americanization* (see References).

In "[translation]," the text in the right column are fragments of text from the left-hand column, translated into New Orleans Creole by the author, using the website www.louisianacreoledictionary.com.

"litany in which love remains" is after Richard Siken's poem "Litany in Which Certain Things are Crossed Out."

"a foolish controversy over the color of the skin" takes its title from a quote by poet, journalist, and activist Rodolphe Desdunes, who wrote *Our People and Our History: A Tribute to the Creole People of Color in Memory of the Great Men They Have Given Us and of the Good Works They Have Accomplished.*

In "private school" the italicized lines are lyrics from Handel's *Messiah*, which are taken from Biblical verses.

"privilege reproduces itself" takes its epigraph from the poem "Félicité" by Robin Coste Lewis.

"cartography" takes its epigraph from the poem "The Pickaxe" by Jalal ad-Din Muhammad Rumi.

"archival" is after Monica Youn's poem "Portrait of a Hanged Woman."

"story" is partly inspired by the novel *Blindness* by José Saramago.

References

Alexander, Eleanor. *Lyrics of Sunshine and Shadow: The Tragic Courtship and Marriage of Paul Laurence Dunbar and Alice Ruther Moore.* NYU Press, Sept. 2001.

Brody, Jane E. "Among hyenas, females dominate jittery males." *New York Times,* 1982.

Crair, Ben. "Love the Fig." *New Yorker,* Aug. 10, 2016.

Dunbar-Nelson, Alice Moore. *Violets and Other Tales.* Originally published by *The Monthly Review,* 1895.

Hirsch AR and J Logsdon, eds. *Creole New Orleans: Race and Americanization.* Louisiana State University Press, 1992.

"Historical Sketch of Dunbar High School." Paul Laurence Dunbar Senior High School website. Available at: <https://www.dunbarhsdc.org/history.html>.

Hull, Gloria T., ed. *Give Us Each Day: The Diary of Alice Dunbar-Nelson.* W. W. Norton and Co., 1984.

"In Nation's First Black Public High School, A Blueprint For Reform." National Public Radio, July 29, 2013.

Jones CE et al. "Anthropogenic and geologic influences on subsidence in the vicinity of New Orleans, Louisiana 2016." *Journal of Geophysical Research: Solid Earth,* 2016.

Mathieu family okra gumbo recipe.

Mathieu and Boucrée family oral histories.

Mukherjee, Siddhartha. "Same but different: How epigenetics can blur the line between nature and nurture." *New Yorker,* May 2, 2016.

Simmons, LaKisha. *Crescent City Girls.* UNC Press, 2015.

Acknowledgments

Immense gratitude for the following journals, in which versions of these poems first appeared:

"furnace" in *Underbelly.*

"[translation]" in *Obsidian.* Finalist for the 2017 Gwendolyn Brooks Centennial Poetry Prize.

"astacology" in Moonstone Poetry's 2017 *Anthology of Featured Poets.*

"an easy way of living" in *Bayou Magazine.*

"isthmus" in *Empty Mirror.*

"a foolish controversy over the color of the skin" in *Southern Humanities Review.*

"maron" and "to know a thing" in *Boston Review's* special poetry issue, WHAT NATURE.

"thunder's baby" in *Yemassee Journal.* Winner of the 2017 *Yemassee Journal* Poetry Prize (selected by Jericho Brown). Nominated for the Pushcart Prize.

"privilege reproduces itself" in *Narrative Magazine.*

"archival" in *TriQuarterly.*

"my mother teaches me self-preservation" in *Vinyl Poetry.*

"DCA → SDQ" in *Obra/Artifact.*

"self-portrait as a series of bent zoning laws" in *New Delta Review.*

"still life with pedigree" in *Foundry.* Nominated for *Best of the Net Anthology* 2018.

To my Philly poetry family, whose loving support and poetic discussions have altered many of these poems and me in extraordinary ways: Yolanda Wisher, Trapeta Mayson, Raquel Salas Rivera, Shevaun Brannigan, Raena Shirali, Tim Lynch, Nomi Stone, Daniel Brian Jones, and Alan Beyersdorf. Thank you for pushing me to tell these stories as clearly as I could.

To Kimberly Reyes, my forever Callaloo roommate, whose careful reading and editorial suggestions made this book immeasurably better.

To Alice Moore Dunbar-Nelson, whose life and words inspired many of these poems: thank you for walking with me.

To the many scholars who illuminate the history of New Orleans, especially LaKisha Simmons, Arnold R. Hirsch, and Joseph Logsdon; their works were particularly helpful in my research for this book. A special thanks to LaKisha Simmons for her encouragement and enthusiasm for this project.

To Heather Christle, Alyse Knorr, Kate Partridge, and Matthew Shenoda, whose belief in this book is the reason that you hold it today. Thank you for seeing these stories and for making a space for this book in the world. To Tyehimba Jess, whose insights helped me to refine this book during its final stages.

To my life & love partner, Justin G. Reid, who gave me the idea to write this book in the first place, and whose passion for history and storytelling makes me a better writer and human.

To my family, whose unwavering support has always been the fuel for my dreams. My parents, Cathie and Michael, and my siblings, Jeannette and Benoît, have been witness to my storytelling from the very beginning. Immeasurable gratitude to my grandparents, Owen Rudolph Mathieu, Catherine Merkle Jones Boucrée, and Stanley Anthony Boucrée, whose countless stories form the backbone of this book. Special thanks to my paternal grandmother, Louise Marguerite Llopis Mathieu, who spent many patient hours answering my questions about her life. This book would not exist without those conversations.

And to you, reader: thank you for your curiosity.